Derek Jeter's
You're A Star

with
Ann Farry DeWerth

Illustrations by
Jeff Suntala

To my sister Sharlee, who made this book possible.
To all the kids who have dreams and to their caregivers
and families for nurturing those dreams.
To my parents, always an inspiration.
— Derek Jeter

Published in part due to the generosity of Major League Baseball

Special thanks to: Sharlee Jeter, Creative Consultant, Turn 2 Foundation;
Paula Grooms, George Muller, Ann DeWerth, Hank Czekalinski, Debbie Graham, Terri McNeely, Susan O'Donnell and
Jeff Suntala, IMG Creative; Casey Close and Mary Catherine McCooey, IMG Baseball; Kristin Kiser,
Crown Publishing; Eileen Chambers, Educational Consultant.

Images of Derek Jeter used with permission from photographs by Chuck Solomon/*Sports Illustrated*,
Walter Iooss, Jr., Rich Pilling/MLB Photos, Vincent LaForet/Allsport.
The former originally appeared in *Game Day, My Life On and Off the Field* by Derek Jeter, Crown Publishing.

TURN 2 FOUNDATION, INC.

Copyright 2002 Turn 2 Foundation, Inc. All rights reserved.

Published by IMG Creative, a division of IMG, and The Mark McCormack Group of Companies.

Printed in the United States of America
Printed by Worzalla

Based on Derek Jeter's *10 Life Lessons* and adapted from *The Life You Imagine* by Derek Jeter with Jack Curry, copyright 2000 by Turn 2, Inc.

You're A Star!/Ann Farry DeWerth
Summary: Derek Jeter and a shy star take a magical trip through New York City.

ISBN 1-878843-35-4

Derek Jeter's You're A Star

Far, far away, at the edge of the sky, a shy star tried to shine for the very first time. He huffed and puffed, but all he could muster was a tiny flicker.

"You're no real star," the other stars teased. "You're not even shiny!"

"Am too!" he quivered, blinking back twinkle-dust tears. "Am too."

He would show those mean stars! He would run away to the people-city below. Hello buildings! Hello people! he would shout.

But the buzzing city frightened the bashful star. Hushed by shyness, he didn't say a word.

"I'm not even bright enough to be a street light," he sighed to himself.

The wind, feeling sorry for the star, whispered in a breeze, "I know a sweeter sound. Over there is a happy noise, a place where you can shine super bright."

The star followed the hum.

Suddenly, the star came upon a wondrous sight. Under the cloak of velvet sky lay a dusty diamond wrapped in a glittering ring of people. The star liked the cheering people so much he dangled above until they all marched away and the lights turned off one by one. Soon, only his own single beam danced upon the field.

But someone was still there! A magical man stepped into the halo of light.
With a sparkling smile and dancing eyes, he stood tall and the star could tell
he was a great man. Curious, the bashful star inched closer, for just a peek.
"Who are you?" asked the star, startled to hear himself speak.

The man smiled and said, "My name's Derek."

"You seem so, so, so…great," squeaked out the star. "You're more sparkly than me. How do you do it?"

"If you want to be great, you need to set your goals high," answered Derek. "Think big. Work hard and make your dreams come true."

"Oh," said the star. "Do you think I could learn to shine brighter? Could I learn how to be a great, shiny, sparkly star? You know, the kind they sing about."

Derek smiled again. "Sure! I've got an idea. Let's take a trip through the city. I have a surprise — a special friend for you to meet. But you have to promise me one thing. You must light the way!"

"Do you think I can do it?" asked the star.

"I know you can," said Derek.

"What if we get lost?" asked the star.
"Don't worry," Derek said. "We can ask him for directions."
"Why would you ask him for help?"
"When you're unsure, find a leader to guide you."

So Derek asked, "Officer, can you help us? We're going to visit a special friend."

"I know just where you're going," the officer said with a grin. "And you're on the right road."

They soon came to a place the star had never seen before.
So many nice people! So many smiling faces! So many amazing animals!
The shy star did not say hello to any of them.
"Come on, Star," Derek said. "It's OK. You can say hello."
"No one will like me," said the star.
"Why not?" asked Derek.
"They'll tease me because I don't always shine my brightest."

Derek smiled. "Everyone gets teased sometimes, even picked on. It's part of growing up. It's called growing pains and everyone has them."

"Even you?" asked the star.

"Even me!" Derek said.

The star puffed himself up, feeling a bit shinier, knowing that Derek understood. "Let's go," said the star.

Like a garden it was, awash in colors and lights. People fluttered about, laughing and talking and waving.

"Where are we?" asked the star. "What is this place?"

"Harlem!" said Derek.

"Hey, there are some of my friends," Derek said. "It's important to have nice friends. To have positive people around you. You know, like having a supporting cast. And guess what?"

"What?"

"Sometimes your family is the strongest supporting cast of all. They guide you when you need help."

The star thought about his family and how much they loved him and he began to shine a bit brighter.

"Come on, Derek," he said. "Let's keep going to meet your special friend. I'll lead the way."

On the next street, a wonderful smell waltzed right into their noses.

"That's the best smell ever. What is it?" asked the star.

"Hot dogs! Want one?" Derek asked. But before the star could answer, he noticed a lonely-looking man sitting on the sidewalk.

"Spare change?" said the man in a lonely-looking voice.

The star was confused.
"Why does that man need money?"
"He's hungry," Derek answered. "It's hard to shine your brightest when the world's unfair."
The star thought for a moment.
"Well, let's buy him a hot dog," he said.
"Great idea," said Derek.
So they did, and the star's heart had to grow a whole inch bigger to let in the happiness he felt, and he burned a bit brighter too.

Don't Be Afraid To Fail

Soon they came to a lanky, swanky street. The star felt lost again. "Maybe this was another city," he thought! Sparkly ladies, limousines! A glossy man in a bright red coat with glossy buttons noticed the star looked bothered. He waved his crisp white glove, saying to Derek and the star, "May I help you?"

"We're going to visit a special friend," answered the star. "And we're a bit lost."

"Ahhhh. I know just the way to go. But it's not easy. Turn left, then right, go upstairs, downstairs, across the street and under a bridge. Go all the way up, all the way down and around some more."

"Do you think that's too hard for us?" asked the star.

"No," said Derek. "Even though it's hard, we can do it. We don't have to be afraid to fail. We'll keep going!"

"And I'll keep leading the way," chimed in the star, and he burned brighter still.

Off they went, beneath a veil of moonlit sky alongside a great, greeny place whose trees peeked over its gate, as if to invite them in.

Just as the star wished he could enter the mysterious forest, a cheery voice called, "Would you like a carriage ride?"

"Yes!" Derek said, and they climbed in the carriage.

They clip-clopped along until they came to a lovely stone wall. There, they saw some boys and girls spraying graffiti! The children were laughing very hard. "Do you think I could shine my light for them? I'm burning brighter now."

"No," Derek said. "You can't do something just because someone else is doing it and it seems like fun. That could be trouble! You have to think before you act."

"But wouldn't I be shinier if I did?"

"No, you wouldn't," said Derek. "That's a bad choice. It ruins our city, and besides, you should use your light for good things, like to keep on lighting our way."

And so he did.

Broadway! Times Square! People poured out of theaters and into the streets. Taxis, horns honking, whizzing by in such a New York hurry that the star grew so dizzy he didn't know what to do! And then they heard a peaceful melody drifting over the noise — a violin sounding soft songs into the night, sharing happy music.
  The star sighed. "I wish I could be good at something like that," he said.

"You can," Derek said. "All you have to do is practice. When people are good at something, it's because they practice. Be serious about what you do, but still have fun."

The star twinkled a nod.

Time to go. Their special friend was waiting.

Soon, a sidewalk bubbling with life. Students, actors, waiters, janitors, artists, barbers, dancers, writers, teachers, people of every sort — Greenwich Village!

"Where should we go now, Derek?" cried the star, wrinkled with worry.

"Let's ask those men playing chess," Derek said.

Puffing up his courage, the star said, "Excuse me sir, can you show us the way downtown?"

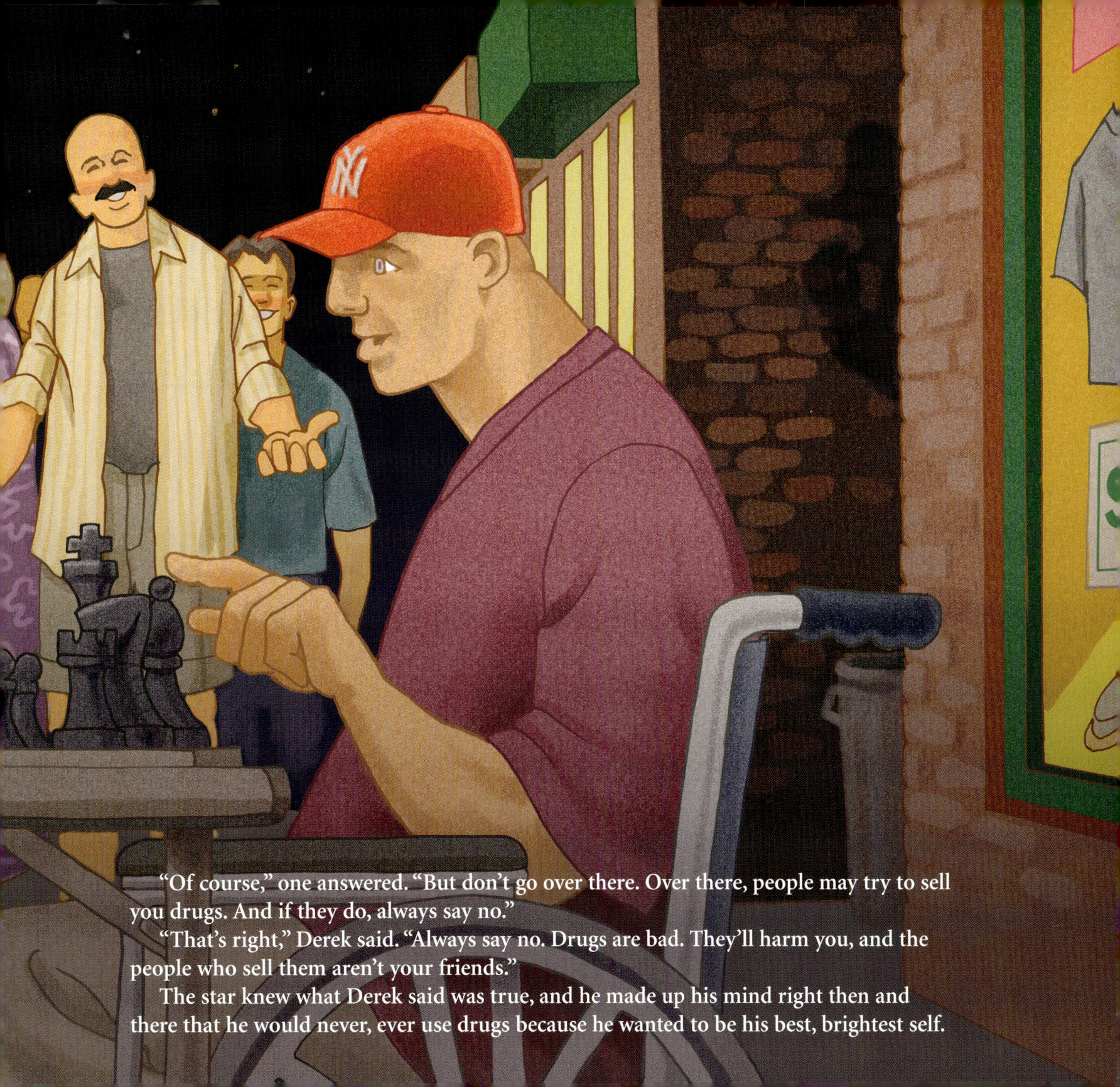

"Of course," one answered. "But don't go over there. Over there, people may try to sell you drugs. And if they do, always say no."

"That's right," Derek said. "Always say no. Drugs are bad. They'll harm you, and the people who sell them aren't your friends."

The star knew what Derek said was true, and he made up his mind right then and there that he would never, ever use drugs because he wanted to be his best, brightest self.

Suddenly, a flash of red rocketed down the street!

"Derek, what's that?" cried the star. "I want to be like that!"

"A fire truck," said Derek. "And those are my friends at the firehouse. They are role models to many boys and girls."

"What's a role model?" asked the star.

"Ask our friend the firefighter," Derek said.

"A role model is someone who sets a good example," answered the smiling firefighter.
"Do you have a role model?"
The star thought for a minute.
"Well, my family shines very brightly in the sky, and they help falling stars too," answered the star who burned a little brighter at the thought.
"Say goodbye to the firefighters," Derek said. "We have to catch the ferry. Our special friend is still waiting."

Derek and the star hopped on the ferry just in time.
As they glided through the harbor, an inky shadow darkened the water. The star shivered.
"Don't be scared," the ferry captain said. "I bring many people to see her every day."
"Who?" cried the star excitedly. "Who are we going to see?"
"There," said the boatman. "Your special friend. There."

Like a mountain of kindness, she rose out of the water.
Her torch touched the sky as her face smiled down upon them in the light of the bashful star.
"Tell us please, what does it take to be great?" Derek asked the lady. "The star and I journeyed a long way to hear what you'll say."
A gentle voice like a warm summer night answered, "The tired, the poor — it says so right here — those that came before, they are great. The people of this city are great. But most of all, people who are kind and good are great."

"Can I be great too?" asked the star.

"You're already great," Liberty answered. "You're a star. You guide people through darkness. You give them something to wish upon and their hopes are reflected in your beaming smile."

"Me?" said the star very slowly. "Great? How?"

"Because you've burned so brightly learning all your lessons," she said. "And don't forget, you led the way."

"It's hard, I know," Derek added. "Life's a daily challenge. But you did it."

The star thought of his family and how they often tried to teach him the same lessons that Derek had, and all at once he longed to be home. He wasn't afraid of the other stars teasing him anymore.

"Thank you Derek," he said. "Goodbye Derek. Goodbye Ms. Liberty." And he floated home to his family in the sky.

Liberty smiled and said, "Derek, I think you've done something wonderful."

"I didn't do it," Derek said. "He did it. Now he's bright enough to lead the other stars."

The next evening, electricity pulsed in the air as the Boys of Summer took the field. Waiting for his turn to bat, Derek felt just as excited as the first time he played. But he wondered what had happened to his friend the star.

"Batter-up!" yelled the umpire, waking Derek from his thoughts. A hush came over the crowd as he stepped up to the plate. He looked up and was amazed to see a dazzling light, a light far brighter than any stadium light. A light almost as bright as the sun!

Derek recognized the sparkling star — his friend the star — hugging everyone in a glorious glow! Now he was certain the star had learned his lessons well, because never, ever had there been such a great, beautiful, shiny star.

"I knew you could do it," Derek exclaimed. "The brightness was inside you all along. You just needed help finding it.

"You're a real star."

You're A Star!

For Grown-Ups and Children

See if you can find Derek's Life Lessons written in the pictures.

Talk about each life lesson.

Talk about how those life lessons can help you.

Talk about making choices and the impact those decisions can make on the future.

Ask your children what they'd like to be when they grow up.
    Talk about what they might do to become what they want.
    Talk about how working hard in school is important.

Talk about all the heroes in the book.
    Discuss how they help people.
    Discuss how you and your child can help people.
    Talk about what it means to be a leader.

Talk about what it means to respect people and value them.

Discuss any new words your child may have learned from reading the story.